AH

DESTINATION DULUTH

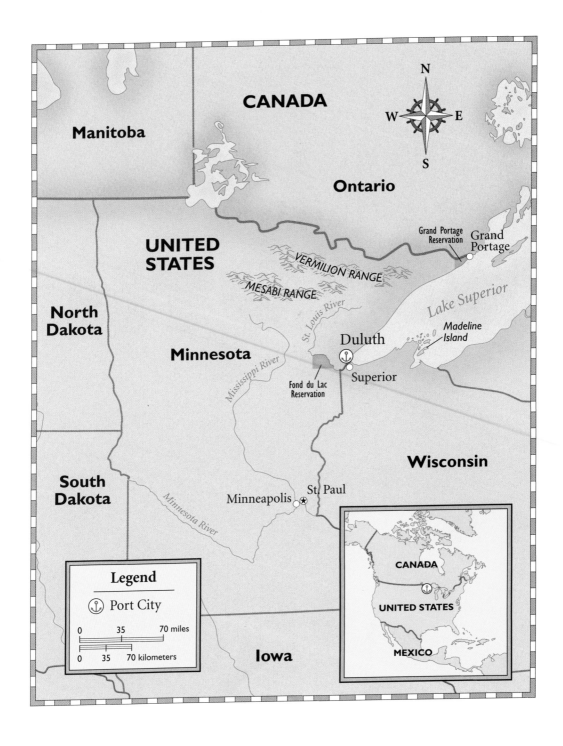

DESTINATION
DULUTH

by Martin Hintz

Lerner Publications Company • Minneapolis

PHOTO ACKNOWLEDGMENTS

Cover photograph by Bob Firth. All inside photos courtesy of Duluth Convention and Visitor's Bureau, pp. 5, 72, 73 (top); © Peter Ford, pp. 6, 9, 15 (top), 17 (top), 42, 46, 51 (top), 53, 55, 56, 73 (bottom), 74; © Sam Alvar, pp. 10, 12, 13 (bottom), 17 (bottom), 47, 54, 57, 60, 64, 65, 66 (bottom), 70 (top), 71 (top); © Tim Slattery, pp. 13 (top), 21, 51 (middle and bottom), 59 (top); photos by Peter Ford courtesy of U.S. Army Corps of Engineers' Lake Superior Marine Museum, pp. 15 (bottom), 34, 38, 39 (bottom), 41; © Patrick Lapinsky, p. 18; Martin Hintz, pp. 19, 49, 52, 58, 69; courtesy of the Seaway Port Authority of Duluth, pp. 20, 40; © Bob Firth, pp. 18 (inset), 22, 28 (top), 63 (top), 68, 70 (bottom); courtesy of the University of Michigan Museum of Anthropology, p. 24; Minnesota Historical Society, pp. 25 (bottom), 27, 28 (bottom), 29, 32, 33, 35 (both), 36, 37, 39 (top), 63 (bottom); Edward E. Ayre Collection, Newberry Library, p. 25 (top); © Penrod/Hiawatha Co., p. 31; Minneapolis Public Library and Information Center, p. 45 (top); courtesy of Matthew Spears, p. 45 (bottom); © Jerry Hennen, p. 59 (bottom); © Kay Shaw, pp. 66 (top), 71 (bottom). Maps by Ortelius Design.

LIBRARY OF CONGRESS CATALOGING-IN-PUBLICATION DATA

Hintz, Martin.
    Destination Duluth / by Martin Hintz.
      p. cm. — (Port cities of North America)
    Includes index.
    Summary: An introduction to the port city of Duluth describing its geography, history, economy, and day-to-day life.
    ISBN 0-8225-2783-9 (lib. bdg. : alk. paper)
    Duluth (Minn.) — Juvenile literature. [1. Duluth (Minn.)]
I. Title. II. Series.
F614.D8H56 1997
977.6'771—dc20   96-14740

Manufactured in the United States of America
1 2 3 4 5 6 – JR – 02 01 00 99 98 97

The glossary that begins on page 76 gives definitions of words shown in **bold type** in the text.

CONTENTS

CHAPTER ONE

LAY OF THE LAND

Fourth of July fireworks shoot high over the Aerial Lift Bridge (facing page), *Duluth's most famous landmark. The lift bridge is the world's fastest and it was built almost entirely of steel from Minnesota's Iron Range.*

One of the longest and narrowest cities in the United States, Duluth stretches 23 miles along the shore of Lake Superior. On stormy days, freezing black waves crash against the city's granite cliffs, sending spray high into the air. But on warm, spring days or during summer's calm, the lake laps gently against the shore. Sailboats bob off the coast, while huge freight ships plow through Duluth's inner harbor toward the port's giant docks.

Location ➤ Located at the far western rim of Lake Superior, Duluth is the fourth largest city in Minnesota, a state in the Upper Midwest. Minnesota is bordered by the Canadian provinces of Ontario and Manitoba to the north and on the west by

North and South Dakota. Iowa lies to the south, and Wisconsin is to the east. Lake Superior forms Minnesota's northeastern boundary, known as the North Shore.

The world's largest body of freshwater in area, Lake Superior is one of the five Great Lakes. This chain—which also includes Lakes Michigan, Huron, Erie, and Ontario—is linked to the Atlantic Ocean by the Great Lakes-St. Lawrence Seaway System. Ships can travel between Duluth and the Atlantic Ocean in about eight days. The 2,342-mile route connects the interior of the North American continent to the rest of the world, making the Great Lakes region one of the largest industrial areas in all of North America.

◀ **The Great Lakes**

Ocean-faring vessels can deliver cargo from across the Atlantic as far inland as Duluth using the interconnected bodies of water that make up the Great Lakes-St. Lawrence Seaway System.

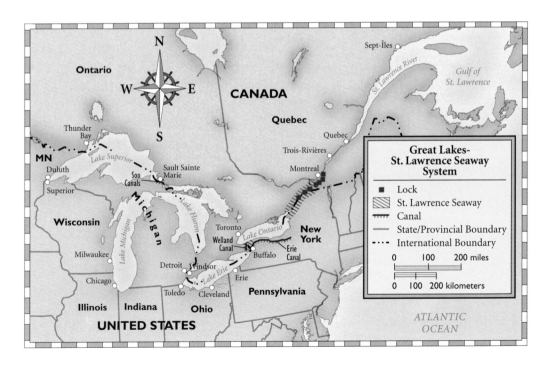

*Skyline Parkway offers the best view of the city and of the sand **spit** called Minnesota Point. High above the lake, Skyline Parkway was the shoreline of what is now Lake Superior about 10,000 years ago.*

The city of Duluth was originally built in the valley that lies between the Lake Superior waterfront and a ridge rising about 800 feet at its highest point. Skyline Parkway, a 30-mile road that runs along the ridge, offers a panoramic view of Duluth and the lake. The downtown business district stretches along the shore, while residential areas creep up the hill. You could say that Duluth's head is in the clouds and its feet dangle in the water.

Duluth's hilly landscape can cause headaches for railroaders. Several diesel engines are necessary to pull heavily loaded train cars up the steep incline from the lake port. Going down the slope is also an experience. Just imagine a 164-car train loaded with 9,000 pounds of taconite easing over the ridge and coming downtown. Train crews are naturally concerned about their brakes!

Skyline Parkway was once the shoreline of Lake Superior, which was formed thousands of years ago by giant masses of ice called glaciers. The ice scraped across the land, scooping out a basin that gradually filled with water as the glaciers melted. Over time the water level

9

dropped and remains at about 600 feet above sea level.

After the heavy glaciers melted, the ground underneath the lake rebounded, causing water to pile up at one end and overflow. The overflow covered the mouth of the St. Louis River, which enters Lake Superior just south of Duluth, and helped create the city's deep, natural harbor. Duluth shares this harbor with its sister city, Superior, Wisconsin. Together Duluth and Superior are known as the Twin Ports.

Minnesota Point, a 6.5-mile sand spit formed by the current of the St. Louis River, extends from Duluth toward the city of Superior. This natural breakwater protects the inner harbor from the raging waters of Lake Superior. A natural opening in Minnesota Point allows ships into the Superior side of the Twin Ports. Vessels enter the Duluth Harbor through a narrow ship canal, which was dug through the Point in 1871.

A brick lighthouse on Minnesota Point once helped guide ships safely through fog and darkness into the harbor. But modern ships rely on advanced radar technology and better lighting systems at the entrances to get them into the Twin Ports. This technology is especially useful during fierce storms. Rough waves and high winds on Lake Superior can be even more dangerous than nasty weather on the open ocean. Hundreds of vessels, from small craft to giant freighters, have sunk to the lake's icy depths.

A Great Lakes freighter enters the ship canal as it leaves the Duluth Harbor. Winds and crosscurrents make navigating the canal tricky business.

The question of weather is on many people's minds when it comes to shipping in Minnesota. Visions of blustery, cold days often come to

◀ **Duluth's Climate**

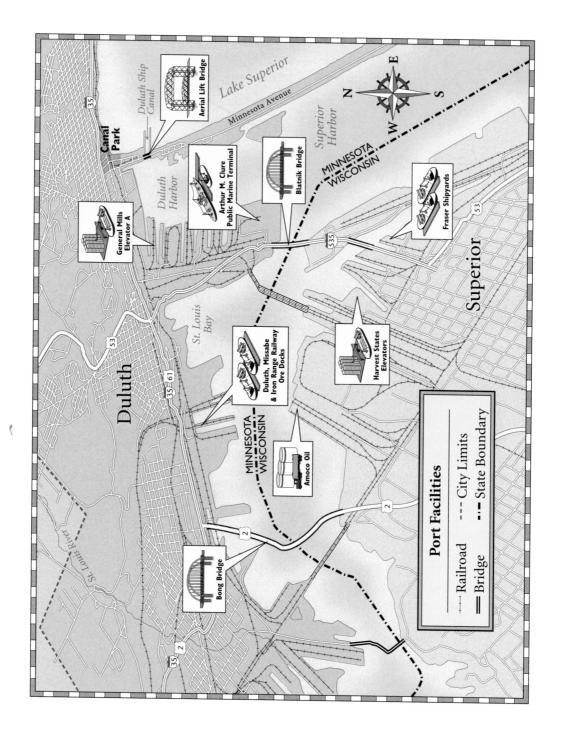

Lake Superior

Duluth Ship Canal

Minnesota Avenue

Superior Harbor

Canal Park

Aerial Lift Bridge

Duluth Harbor

Arthur M. Clure Public Marine Terminal

Blatnik Bridge

MINNESOTA
WISCONSIN

Fraser Shipyards

General Mills Elevator A

St. Louis Bay

Duluth

Superior

Duluth, Missabe & Iron Range Railway Ore Docks

Harvest States Elevators

MINNESOTA
WISCONSIN

Amoco Oil

St. Louis River

Bong Bridge

Port Facilities

—— Railroad
--- City Limits
—— Bridge
—·—·— State Boundary

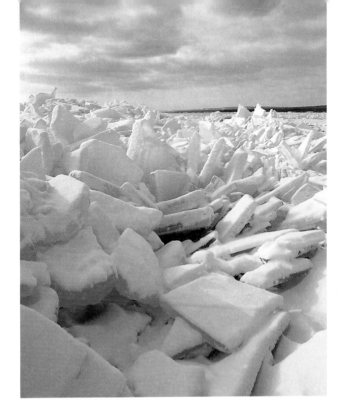

Maneuvering through ice floes (left) *is one of the trickiest aspects of navigating the Great Lakes. A salty, or oceangoing vessel* (facing page, top), *has a specially designed bulbous bow to help protect it from huge, breaking ocean waves. Lakers* (facing page, bottom), *on the other hand, need less protection from waves. They have pointed or rounded bows that are plumb, or vertically straight. This laker follows a path cleared by an icebreaker.*

mind, but in general, Lake Superior has a moderating effect on the climate in Duluth. Winters are warmer and summers are cooler in this city than in much of the rest of the state. Because of the cool breeze coming off the lake in summer, Duluth is sometimes called the Air-Conditioned City. Winters in Duluth are usually dry and cold.

Although Lake Superior never freezes completely, drifting ice is troublesome for ships. To avoid getting icebound in Duluth, lake vessels run from mid-March to mid-January. Oceangoing ships visit the port between the first week of April and mid-December. Early season snows don't affect shipping, but by December and January, large boats called **icebreakers** head out to keep shipping lanes free of drifting ice.

During shipping season, the Port of Duluth serves more than 1,200 vessels, 200 of which are foreign-flag ships. These oceangoing vessels are called salties because they travel through ocean salt water. Great Lakes freighters, or lakers, make up the bulk of the port's business. Many of these ships are 1,000 feet long and can carry up to 68,000 tons of cargo. To accommodate these enormous vessels, workers dredge the harbor bottom, clearing silt and other sediment buildup to maintain a depth of 27 feet. The keels, or bottoms, of the largest ships are only 6 to 12 inches off the harbor floor when fully loaded.

Duluth's Canal Park is located close to the ◀ **Maneuvering through the Port** 1,650-foot-long canal. The Canal Park boardwalk is the best place to watch lakers and salties enter the harbor. As a ship nears the port, it sounds a warning horn. This noise alerts bridge keepers to raise the Aerial Lift Bridge that crosses the 300-foot-wide canal. Motorists who use the bridge to get to Minnesota Point can be bridged, or stopped, for up to 30 minutes as they wait for a ship to pass and the bridge to be lowered.

Pilots—professionals who guide ships into their berths (docking spaces)—must know how to maneuver through the Twin Ports. If the St. Louis River is high, for example, more water is flowing into the lake. Therefore, a ship coming into the port needs to keep its speed to buck the strong current. If the river is low, the current of the lake helps push the ship through the canal, so the pilot has to slow down when entering the port.

As freighters enter the inner harbor, they have to make a sharp, 90-degree turn to the east around a traffic buoy in order to get to the docks on the Superior, Wisconsin, side of the port. Ship captains and pilots use their expertise to navigate through the Twin Ports' 45 miles of water frontage, which includes 17 miles of channels (deep, navigable water routes) and several dozen docks. A heavy ship is difficult to manage, so pilots try to do as little maneuvering as possible.

The Twin Port facilities reflect the types of goods that move through the harbor. Duluth and Superior handle mainly bulk cargo, which includes grain and other dry goods that can be

➤ Duluth ranks as the largest port on the Great Lakes.

➤ Some of the sand that dredging crews bring up from the Duluth Harbor is sold to construction companies.

➤ Lake Superior is the largest body of freshwater in the world.

➤ From east to west, Lake Superior stretches 350 miles. From north to south, the lake covers 160 miles. At its deepest point, the lake reaches 1,333 feet). Offshore in the Duluth area, Lake Superior is about 700 feet deep.

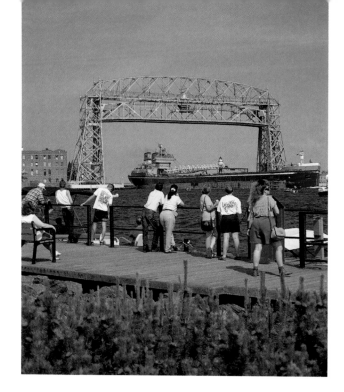

Onlookers can get a great view of the Aerial Lift Bridge in action (right) *from the boardwalk of Canal Park. This early photograph* (below) *shows General Mills Elevator A in the late 1800s.*

piled loosely in a ship. General cargo includes heavy equipment and other products. More than 35 million tons of bulk and prepackaged general cargo move through the Twin Ports each year.

Six grain elevator systems line Duluth's harbor. The tall, cement buildings store wheat, corn, soybeans, barley, and other grains harvested in Minnesota and neighboring states, such as North and South Dakota, Nebraska, Iowa, and Wisconsin. Most of these terminal elevators are more than 100 feet tall and hold more than 1 million bushels of grain. General Mills Elevator A—the oldest active grain elevator in Duluth— was built in 1896. It holds 3.5 million bushels of grain. A more modern facility, Harvest States Cooperatives towering grain terminal can store up to 18 million bushels of grain.

THE RUFFE PROBLEM

In 1987 a small, warm-water fish called the Eurasian ruffe was first reported in the Duluth-Superior harbor. Scientists were alarmed at its quick spread to other areas along the shore of Lake Superior. They feared the prickly little newcomer would edge out fish species native to the lake.

Experts believe the exotic fish hitchhiked to Minnesota in a freighter's **ballast tanks** (loaded tanks that provide stability at sea), which were filled overseas and then flushed into Lake Superior at the end of the journey. In January 1993, various members of the maritime commercial industry from Canada and the United States met in Duluth to discuss the growing problem. Officials established a voluntary ballast water-control program.

As a result of the water-control program, ships bound for the Twin Ports must discharge their ballast tanks well offshore in deep, cold lake water, where ruffe aren't able to survive. Many ships are also fitted with screens across the ballast intake grid to prevent large ruffe from entering the tanks.

But water is never completely removed from the ballast tanks. Water sometimes pools at the bottom of the tanks, allowing some fry (immature fish) to survive and potentially escape into another lake. Although the ruffe problem was taken care of in Lake Superior, for example, the fish were found in Lakes Michigan and Huron in 1995. Because challenges remain, scientists continue to search for additional solutions to the ruffe problem to protect the variety of fish life in the Great Lakes.

Trains carry nearly 60 percent of the grain coming into the port. Tracks bring the loaded railroad cars right up to the docks, where they are unloaded either directly onto a ship or into a grain elevator. Thousands of railcars are unloaded each year in Duluth. With modern machinery, a 3,600-bushel **hopper car** can be emptied automatically in 90 seconds, and within 3 minutes, all the grain is stored. Different grades of grain with varying moisture contents and baking qualities need to be stored in separate bins. Computers keep track of all this activity.

Another major raw material shipped from Duluth is taconite, a type of iron ore mined at

Soybeans are loaded aboard a freighter (top). *Grain cleaning and bagging facilities contribute to making Duluth the largest mover of agricultural commerce on the Great Lakes. Trains and trucks* (above) *bring about 225 million bushels of grain each year to Duluth from farms across the Midwest.*

17

the nearby Mesabi Range in northeastern Minnesota. Dock Number 6, owned by the Duluth, Missabe & Iron Range Railway, is among the largest taconite loading facilities on the Great Lakes. The dock is 2,304 feet long and 85 feet tall. Only 70 employees are needed to operate the maze of conveyor belts that load the taconite.

Dock Number 6 can unload four trains every eight hours on its three tracks. The cars dump the taconite through belly holes directly into storage bins on the dock. Each of these dock pockets holds four cars' worth of taconite—about 280 tons. To fill a 1,000-foot freighter, 875 carloads are needed. This job takes about seven hours.

Ore can be loaded aboard a ship in one of two ways. By means of pure gravity, ore rattles down a chute into a ship's holds (below). *A new loading device was installed at the ore docks to fill bigger and wider ships. The new system includes a moving conveyor belt that evenly distributes heavy loads. Taconite pellets* (inset) *are made from a low-grade iron ore.*

Millions of tons of coal from Montana also pass through the Port of Duluth-Superior every year. The coal arrives by train and is quickly transferred to 1,000-foot-long bulk cargo vessels at rates of up to 11,500 tons per hour. The low-sulphur coal is then transported to midwestern power plants, where it is used as fuel to generate electricity.

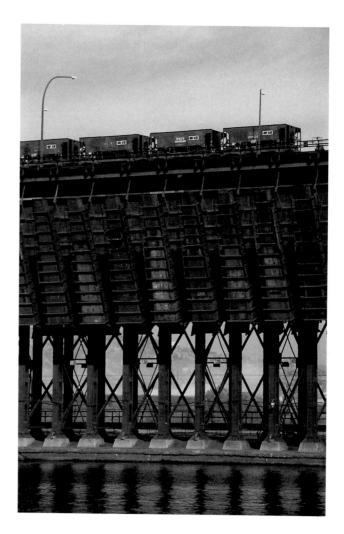

Trains carrying coal or taconite ride right up on the dock to dump their loads into bins. Dock Number 6, nearly half a mile long, can store up to 150,000 tons of taconite ore.

Many general cargo ships dock at the Arthur M. Clure Public Marine Terminal, a sprawling facility owned by the Seaway Port Authority of Duluth. The Clure Terminal has 6,600 feet of berths, where up to seven vessels can dock at a time. The terminal has loading and unloading facilities for ships, railroad cars, and trucks. Special transfer equipment can move cargo on pallets or in slings, and two muscular, rail-mounted **gantry cranes** work together to lift up to 150 tons. These capabilities allow large, heavy goods, including machinery and building materials, to move efficiently through the port. A roll-on–roll-off ramp enables containers

A 272,810-pound cylinder tested the limits of this pair of gantry cranes. The Port of Duluth provides modern equipment and shoreside assistance for docked vessels.

The port's roll-on–roll-off ramp makes loading and unloading containerized cargo easy. Trucks can drive right off the ship with a full trailer and head straight to the interstate.

on wheels, such as truck trailers, to be driven on or off a ship.

Shippers can keep goods at the Clure Terminal's storage facilities. These storage facilities include 300,000 square feet of space enclosed by fireproof steel and concrete, as well as 500,000 square feet of open storage space. This total storage capacity is equal to about eight average-size ships. Bagging facilities at the terminal package grain and other bulk goods before they are loaded onto cargo ships. The Clure Terminal also includes a **free trade zone** (FTZ), where goods can be stored or used to make other goods without paying U.S. customs duties (taxes on imports).

With grain terminals and ships visible from many parts of the city, people in Duluth don't forget they live near a harbor. Each day at noon, a giant foghorn sounds the time. Every 52 seconds during foggy nights, the horn also speaks. The resonant bellow can't be missed. "It's like living in a lighthouse," the locals joke.

CHAPTER TWO

DULUTH'S HISTORY

Duluth's Earliest Inhabitants ▶ Known as Paleo-Indians, nomadic hunters from northeastern Asia tracked elk, deer, and mastodons (large, elephantlike animals) to the thick pine forests of what is now Minnesota about 10,000 years ago, if not earlier. Some groups camped along the North Shore, attracted by the abundance of wild animals and the clear, fish-filled waters of Lake Superior. The Paleo-Indians skillfully chipped flint and other stones into spearheads and arrow points for weapons.

Eastern Archaic peoples of the Copper Culture lived in the Great Lakes region between 5000 B.C. and 1000 B.C. They camped in one place for long periods of time if the fishing and hunting were good. Descended from the Paleo-Indians,

The crystal clear waters and thick forests of the North Shore (facing page) *were abundant hunting and fishing grounds for the area's earliest Native populations.*

23

This arrowhead is evidence of the early inhabitants of what is now Minnesota.

these people crafted weapons and tools from copper, a metal found throughout the Great Lakes region. Copper was easy to smelt, or melt, to shape into fishhooks, harpoon points, spearheads, and other tools. Eastern Archaic peoples also improved on the stone-carving techniques of their predecessors, using more advanced grinding and polishing methods.

Peoples of the Northeast Woodland Culture lived throughout what is now the northeastern United States between 1000 B.C. and A.D. 1600. The dense forests near Lake Superior were a source of shelter, tools, and fuel for some of these Woodland groups. Fishers pulled sturgeon and whitefish from the lake, while hunters preyed on deer and elk as the animals drank the clear water. Gatherers harvested wild rice in reedy marshes and picked berries that grew in the woods. The stable food supply enabled Woodland groups in the Lake Superior region to build permanent villages.

By the 1600s, the Dakota and the Ojibwa (who also call themselves the Anishinabe)—two

◄ The Dakota and the Ojibwa

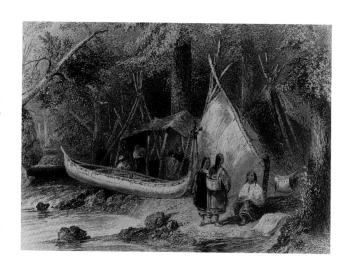

The plentiful forests and complex network of waterways of what is now northern Minnesota were important to the Ojibwa (right) *and Dakota peoples* (below). *These resources provided the tribes with shelter, food, and means of transportation.*

groups descended from the Woodland Culture—were living in what is now Minnesota. The Dakota were expert hunters who tracked game through the woods west and south of Lake Superior. In grassy river valleys, they built permanent villages of bark-covered houses.

The Ojibwa migrated from the east to the shores of Lake Superior and established a permanent camp at La Pointe (what is now Madeline Island) off the northwestern coast of present-day Wisconsin. Lake Superior served as a highway for the Ojibwa, whose sturdy birch canoes could visit every inlet, island, and peninsula. Some Ojibwa settled near where the St. Louis River meets Lake Superior, a place they called Head of the Lake. From there the Indians could fish in the river rapids, hike inland to hunt or to harvest maple sap for syrup, and still have easy access to Lake Superior. The big encampment at La Pointe was less than 100 miles away, making it easy to return for trade, council gatherings, and celebrations.

From their lodges at Head of the Lake, the Ojibwa fanned out. But by moving deep into the pine forests west of Lake Superior, they ran headlong into the Dakota people. When the two groups met, fighting erupted over control of rich hunting grounds.

At the same time, French traders began travel- ◀ **The Fur Trade**
ing to the area to trap and to trade furs. The rivers and lakes of the eastern Great Lakes region were already major trade routes dotted with outposts. At these posts, traders offered manufactured goods to the area's Native groups in exchange for furs, which were in high demand in Europe.

The first European to reach the westernmost point of Lake Superior was Daniel Greysolon, Sieur du Lhut. Born in 1636 in France, Sieur du Lhut was a trader and explorer. His goal was to find a water passage across North America to Asia and to help make this wilderness route safe for European trade and settlement.

Sieur du Lhut worked hard to stop the warfare between the Dakota and the Ojibwa, figuring that there would be better trading opportunities for the French if the fighting ended. In 1679, at a peace meeting held near Head of the Lake (called Fond du Lac in French), he convinced both Indian groups to sign a treaty recognizing the authority of French King Louis XIV.

The treaty made the Ojibwa go-betweens for the French and the Dakota. Under the agreement, the Ojibwa were allowed access to the Dakotas' rich hunting grounds. The Dakota, in turn, were assured of a constant source of

> ➤ *Dakota* means "friend" or "ally" in the Dakota language.

> ➤ In the Ojibwa's language, *Anishinabe* means "first people." And *Ojibwa* refers to a puckered seam in the moccasins the Ojibwa wore.

> ➤ Sieur du Lhut hoped to find a water passage across North America that would link the Atlantic to the Pacific Ocean. Such a route was eventually discovered far north of the Great Lakes. The Northwest Passage—which winds its way through icy Arctic waters—was fully navigated for the first time in 1906.

Duluth is named after French explorer Daniel Greysolon, Sieur du Lhut. In 1679 du Lhut convinced the Dakota and Ojibwa Indians to sign a treaty giving the French better fur-trading opportunities.

DANIEL GREYSOLON SIEUR DULHUT
AT THE HEAD OF THE LAKES — 1679

European trade goods. Trade on Lake Superior increased as the Ojibwa paddled canoes loaded with pelts to Grand Portage—the lake's principal trading post located 150 miles to the northeast. The Ojibwa traders returned with wool blankets, steel pots, muskets, colored cloth, and other items.

The calm did not last long, however. By 1736 continued disputes over tribal territory led to fierce fighting, initiating another 50 years of warfare between the Ojibwa and the Dakota. The Ojibwa eventually took over the entire northern half of what is now Minnesota. Some

This reconstructed eighteenth-century fur-trading post (above) *is located in Grand Portage, Minnesota, just south of the Canadian border. Two fur traders* (right) *pose for their portrait.*

Dakota remained in the region to continue battling the Ojibwa, but most fled their woodland homes for life on the vast plains to the west.

In the meantime, many Indian groups in the British and the French colonies to the east were forced to choose sides in the French and Indian War, which was fought between 1754 and 1763. When the British defeated the French, authority over the hunting grounds and trade routes of the Great Lakes region passed to the British.

Throughout the late 1700s and early 1800s, the Ojibwa continued to provide furs to traders working for the Hudson's Bay Company and the North West Company. American entrepreneur John Jacob Astor recognized the value of commerce on Lake Superior. In 1817 he established a post at Fond du Lac for his new American Fur Company.

Continued warfare between the Ojibwa and **◄ Treaties**
the remaining Dakota disrupted the lucrative business of U.S. traders. In 1826 U.S. representatives and Ojibwa leaders signed the Treaty of Fond du Lac, which established boundaries between Native lands. The treaty also gave the U.S. government the right to mine in Ojibwa territory.

By the mid-1830s, the demand for furs had dropped in Europe, and trading companies began shutting down their posts. As the fur trade declined, the mining industry started to boom in the Great Lakes region. After a geological survey in the late 1840s confirmed the existence of both copper and iron deposits in the Ojibwa lands near Head of the Lake, prospectors began pressuring the government to open this region for white settlement.

A series of treaties between the U.S. government and Indian leaders gradually picked away at Ojibwa territory around Lake Superior. Weighing heavily in favor of government demands, the treaties slowly pried open Native lands for settlement.

Eager prospectors, lured by the possibility of finding copper, flooded into Wisconsin and Minnesota, both of which had gained statehood by the 1850s. Superior was laid out by George R. Stuntz in 1854. On Minnesota Point, Stuntz built a house, a dock, and a warehouse—the beginnings of a port settlement.

By this time, the Soo Canals were being built between Lakes Superior and Huron. **Locks** in the canals would allow large freight and passenger ships to bypass rough rapids. Vessels would then be able to travel from busy eastern

30

> In 1859 a scarlet fever epidemic hit Duluth and nearly wiped out the city's population.

> The Minnesota Point Lighthouse was named to the National Register of Historic Places in 1975. The lighthouse was in use from 1859 until 1878. During foggy weather, lighthouse keepers would blow for hours into a tin horn in order to let crews know how close they were to shore.

and midwestern ports such as Buffalo, Cleveland, Detroit, and Chicago all the way to Head of the Lake. With the prospect of this new ease in transportation, U.S. legislators gave in to the pressure to open Ojibwa lands in Minnesota.

In late 1854, more than 5,000 Ojibwa and their leaders met with government officials at La Pointe. The government representatives asked the Ojibwa to surrender all their territory north and west of Lake Superior. After two weeks of negotiations, Ke-che-waish-ke, leader of the La Pointe Band of Ojibwa, and 84 other tribal leaders eventually agreed to sign the Treaty of La Pointe. In exchange for ceding their land to the U.S. government, the Ojibwa received $5,000 in coins and $8,000 in trade goods annually for the following 20 years. Many Ojibwa were pushed onto the Grand Portage and Fond du Lac Reservations, lands that the U.S. government set aside for the Indians.

A ship passes through the Soo Canals, which connect Lakes Superior and Huron. Construction on the canal was finished in 1955. Ships traveling the Seaway System from the Atlantic Ocean to Duluth end up 600 feet higher than where they entered.

With the Treaty of La Pointe signed, prospectors and developers poured over the Minnesota border from Wisconsin. Each wanted to grab the best chunk of land. Eleven different townsites were laid out, all of which were eventually folded within one city. In 1856 settlers named the site after the explorer Sieur du Lhut, using the English spelling—Duluth.

Docks, stores, warehouses, hotels, saloons, and government offices sprang up in the new city. Although workers had built a narrow, rough road from St. Paul (the state's capital) in southern Minnesota to Lake Superior, most people still preferred water routes, which the region depended on for food and trade goods.

◄ Growth of Duluth (1800s)

Shantytowns sprang up around Duluth in the 1850s. They were inhabited by people seeking work in the mines and in the growing port city.

3000 **LABORERS**

WANTED

On the *LAKE SUPERIOR AND MISSISSIPPI RAILROAD from Duluth at the Western Extremity of Lake Superior, to ST PAUL*

Constant Employment will be given.   Wages range from $2.00 to $4.00 per Day.

MECHANICS
Are Needed at Duluth!

Wages to Masons and Plasterers, $4.00 per day; Carpenters, $3.00 per day.

10,000 **EMIGRANTS**

WANTED TO SETTLE ON THE LANDS OF THE COMPANY, NOW OFFERED ON LIBERAL CREDITS AND AT LOW PRICES.

Large bodies of Government Lands, subject to *Homestead* Settlement, or open to *Pre-Emption*.   These Lands offer Facilities to Settlers not surpassed, if equalled by any lands in the West.   They lie *right along the line* of the Railroad connecting Lake Superior with the Mississippi River, one of the most important Roads in the West. Forty miles of the Road are now in running order, and the whole Road (150 miles) will be completed by June, 1870.   WHITE and YELLOW PINE, and VALUABLE HARDWOOD, convenient to Market, abound.

The SOIL is admirably adapted to the raising of WINTER WHEAT and TAME GRASSES.   *Stock have Good Pasture until the Depth of Winter.*

This announcement was posted in Duluth on June 14, 1869. Laborers willing to work on the Lake Superior & Mississippi Railroad (L.S. & M.R.R.) were offered $2.00 to $4.00 a day, in addition to company land at low cost and free transportation on the completed railroad.

The population of the entire North Shore area declined when the Civil War (1861–1865) erupted between the northern and southern states. Many people returned to their home states in the eastern United States to be near their families during wartime. Others fled to Canada to avoid being drafted into the military.

When the war ended in 1865, investors began eyeing the vast mineral- and timber-rich lands of the northern Minnesota wilderness. In 1869 Jay Cooke, a financier (financial agent) from Philadelphia, helped fund the building of a railroad track from St. Paul to Head of the Lake. Duluth boomed once again. Soon Cooke's railroad—called the Lake Superior & Mississippi Railroad—was hauling timber south to mills and bringing grain from the western plains to the Port of Duluth for shipment to eastern markets.

The first passenger train arrived in Duluth on August 1, 1870. Thousands of people poured into the area by rail and boat, lured by jobs in the timber and shipping industries. Many others stopped in Duluth before heading west to the vast plains of the Dakotas or south to the rich farmland of Iowa.

As Duluth's population soared, its residents demanded improvements to their side of the harbor. Ships could only get into the safe, inner harbor at Duluth by entering at the eastern end of Minnesota Point, near the city of Superior. Docks and piers built toward Lake Superior on Minnesota Point were being damaged by

Progress is made on the building of the L.S. & M.R.R.

By the 1870s, Duluth's port was booming. This freight depot (top) was the end of the line for much of the timber and grain bound for the Port of Duluth via the L.S. & M.R.R. Upon reaching its destination, grain was stored in Duluth's first grain elevator, General Mills Elevator A (right). Built in 1870, the original Elevator A burned to the ground 16 years later.

high winds and waves, so Duluth residents wanted a canal dug through the point closer to Duluth.

Wisconsinites, however, worried that any improvements made to Duluth's harbor would affect the volume of shipping at their port. For this reason, Superior filed a federal lawsuit in 1871 to halt the dredging of a canal. The U.S. Supreme Court ruled in favor of Wisconsin and ordered that all dredging be stopped.

But before the order could be delivered by a federal marshal, workers had already dug a canal from the lake to the inner harbor. This canal was the forerunner of the main channel that now leads into the terminal area of Duluth.

The opening of the canal kept Duluth booming, and by 1873 more than 5,000 people lived in the city. In the same year, however, Cooke's company collapsed. Cooke had expanded the railroads too quickly and had simply run out of money. This failure led to a panic in Duluth. Businesses that depended on the railroads closed, and residents left in search of new jobs. The population dropped as low as 1,300.

But by the early 1880s, Duluth was well on its way to economic recovery. There were several

By the end of the 1800s, Duluth's economy was improving. Increased shipments of grain and iron ore made the port city a major intersection of trade.

A late nineteenth-century iron mine contributed to the steel production industry.

reasons for the new boom. As farmers settled the lands west of Minnesota, more and more grain came to the port for shipment east. Companies eager to mine the vast iron ore deposits nearby set up their headquarters in Duluth. By the late 1880s, Duluth's population had soared to 33,000.

By 1888, 2,200 ships carrying almost two million tons of cargo annually berthed in Duluth. Ten different railroads served the port. The locks at Sault Ste. Marie were improved in order to allow larger ships into Lake Superior. When the Duluth ore docks were built in 1893, the city soon became a major terminal for ore destined for steel mills in Indiana, Ohio, Michigan, and Illinois.

In the late 1890s, the U.S. Army Corps of Engineers enlarged the Duluth harbor entrance to a width of 300 feet and installed concrete piers that reached out 1,700 feet into the lake. Foundations for the Aerial Lift Bridge were

The predecessor to the Aerial Lift Bridge was constructed in 1905. The bridge's first design included a suspended gondola, big enough to hold six cars, which carried its passengers across the canal. Twenty-five years later, the current model was built with a rising road deck, allowing more traffic to cross.

poured in 1904. Soon this structure arched over the ship canal, connecting the mainland with Minnesota Point.

◀ Duluth in the 1900s

Duluth's rapid development continued throughout the early 1900s. Blast furnaces used ore from the Iron Range to make structural steel. Shipyards turned out barges and freighters. The need for these industries increased during World War I (1914–1918), when Duluth helped supply ships and goods to the war effort in Europe.

Duluth prospered until the 1930s, when the Great Depression hit the city. Many businesses shut down, leaving nearly one-third of the workforce unemployed. Shipment of iron ore dropped by almost 95 percent.

Demand for ore, grain, and new ships soared when World War II (1939–1945) broke out.

> ➤ In 1909 the United States and Canada set up the International Joint Commission to deal with navigation, sanitation, irrigation, recreation, pollution, and other water-use issues affecting the Great Lakes.

Millions of dollars poured into the port community. Even the end of the war did not slow down this economic engine. An all-time record of 58.9 million tons of iron ore went through the harbor in 1953. And when the Iron Range was depleted of high-grade ore, the production of taconite (a low-grade ore) took its place. Taconite and coal from mines in Montana and Wyoming kept the loaded trains pouring into the city.

Workers at Duluth's coal docks pose for a photographer (right) *in the early 1900s. Since that time, fewer workers have been needed to run the port facilities. Duluth's shipyards* (below) *used local ore to make steel for building ships.*

THE RACE IS ON

Captains like to be first. Racing against the weather and setting records is an exciting challenge. A little bit of ice didn't bother the *L/T Argosy.* When the bulk carrier from India arrived in Duluth at 3:18 P.M. on April 1, 1995, it was heralded as the earliest springtime arrival of an oceangoing ship to the Twin Ports since the St. Lawrence Seaway opened in 1959. The mayor of Duluth presented an award to the captain of the *Argosy* for his record-breaking performance.

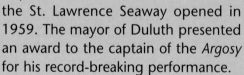

In 1959 the St. Lawrence Seaway opened. This water route enabled oceangoing vessels to reach the Twin Ports, and the harbor front bustled with activity. The Arthur M. Clure Public Marine Terminal was built with berth facilities for ships, on-site rail service, warehouses, and refrigeration units. By this time, Duluth and Superior were working together to bring shipping business to their ports.

Duluth reached its peak in population in the 1960s, with more than 100,000 residents. But

Spectators gather to watch the opening of the St. Lawrence Seaway in 1959. This development allowed oceangoing ships to sail inland from the Atlantic Ocean as far west as Duluth.

by the 1970s, the city was facing many challenges. The shipyards closed, lured by technological advances in other states. Steel plants also shut down, choosing to relocate instead of upgrading their facilities to meet new state environmental regulations.

In the 1980s, the Twin Ports continued to struggle with new challenges. Barge traffic increased down the nearby Mississippi River, carrying more grain to New Orleans, Louisiana, for shipment overseas. Expanded American grain trade with Asia also meant that some of the corn and wheat from the Great Plains states was diverted to ports on the West Coast. From there, the cargo was shipped to Asia across the Pacific Ocean.

Throughout the 1990s, Duluth remained a major cargo transit hub. With changes in the world's trading patterns, however, the Twin Port area economy has had to work to diversify its business. In 1996 a major airline maintenance plant opened in Duluth. This facility includes an 11,000-foot-long runway at Duluth International Airport. The longest in Minnesota, the runway is able to handle giant cargo planes, which require more time on the ground to bring heavy loads to a full stop. New facilities and transportation improvements such as these will help ensure that Duluth and its port remain a vital transportation center into the twenty-first century.

THE TWIN PORTS AT WORK

What is Trade? ➤ Trade is the process of buying and selling goods. It can take place on a small scale, such as trading baseball cards with your neighborhood friends. Trade also occurs on an international scale when countries buy products—such as cars or oil—from one another. People trade because they need or want something that someone else has.

Trade can be an involved, intricate network. For instance, say a farmer in Minnesota raises wheat, and a miner in Montana digs coal. The farmer needs electricity in her barn. The miner would like a sweet roll for his breakfast.

Commerce is still a major part of Duluth's livelihood. Timber (facing page), *transported to the Duluth docks nearby, is shipped to paper mills in Wisconsin, Michigan, and Ohio.*

43

Between these two workers and their needs are **brokers,** who buy and sell items such as coal and wheat. Once the goods are sold, a shipper ensures that the materials get to the right place at the right time. A warehouse operator might then store the raw materials until they can be made into a finished product. Inspectors check the quality of the materials to make sure they meet environmental and health standards. And bankers keep track of all the monetary transactions among these parties.

This interlocking system of trade enables the farmer to light her barn and the miner to have his sweet roll. The wheat that the farmer grows is sold to a mill, which grinds it into flour. The flour might then be shipped to a supplier in Montana, from whom a local baker would buy it to make the miner's sweet roll.

Meanwhile, the miner's coal might be sent by train to a power plant in Minnesota, where it is burned to produce the electricity that lights up the farmer's barn. Both the farmer and the miner got what they needed. That's what trade is all about.

◄ Trade in the Great Lakes Region

Trade is big business in Duluth. The Port of Duluth-Superior is the anchoring link of the Great Lakes region, which is home to more than 90 million people, or about one-fourth of North America's population. About two-thirds of all Canadian industry lies in this area, and almost half of the United States' corn and soybeans is grown here. Forty percent of U.S. manufacturing plants are located in the Great Lakes region. So are five of the nation's top steel-producing states.

All of these businesses depend on the region's ports for trade. More than 40 provincial and interstate highways and 30 railroads hook into ports on the Great Lakes. Together trucks, railcars, and ships keep goods moving through the region to destinations as far away as Europe and Africa.

Ore from this iron mine (right) *near Hibbing, Minnesota, will make its way by railroad to an ore dock in Duluth* (below).

A worker makes repairs on the side of a tugboat damaged by winter ice.

Duluth's port brings a lot of money into the city. For instance, waterfront businesses pay more than $2 million annually in local property taxes. And the salaries earned by employees in local shipping businesses often get spent in Duluth. Altogether the port brings about $240 million to Duluth each year. ◄ **The Port Earns Money**

Yet running a port is not cheap. Millions of dollars are needed to repair and improve docks, buildings, sidewalks, and streets that are within the port's jurisdiction. Funds also go for dredging to maintain the shipping canals. And it costs shipowners a lot of money to keep their fleets in top condition.

Port workers see the benefits of keeping their port in tip-top shape. A well-maintained port keeps ships coming back. Fleet owners appreciate quality accommodations and services offered at a port. If a ship can be quickly and easily loaded or unloaded, the turnaround time in port is shorter. This means the vessel can deliver goods faster and make more money for the shipowner.

More goods—about 40 million tons per year—pass through Duluth-Superior than through any other port on the Great Lakes. About 50 percent of this cargo is iron ore, 30 percent is coal, and 10 percent is grain. The remainder is general cargo. This large volume of cargo puts Duluth-Superior among the nation's top 20 ports.

Imports and Exports ➤ Where do all these raw materials and goods originate? And where do they go? The Seaway Port Authority of Duluth keeps track of the ebb and flow of port traffic. According to their surveys, less than 1 percent of the cargo that moves through the port originates or is consumed in the Twin Port area.

The majority of the Twin Ports' tonnage is taconite, which is mined just west of Duluth on Minnesota's Iron Range. From Duluth, taconite is shipped to steel mills in the lower Great Lakes region. Trains bring coal from Montana to Duluth, where they are unloaded into huge bulk cargo vessels. This coal fuels power plants throughout the Midwest.

Coal cars line up with their cargo just outside the Port of Duluth.

FROM THE FIELD TO THE TABLE

In late August, Farmer Jones steps down from her tractor after harvesting spring wheat from her farm in North Dakota. Soon trucks will come to haul her crop to the grain elevator in town, where it will be poured into covered hopper cars headed for the Port of Duluth.

At the elevator company, grain is poured into hopper cars through the cars' top hatches. The hatches are sealed, as are the gates on the bottom of each car. The train reaches Duluth in three days. At the General Mills dock, the seals are broken and the gates on the bottom of each car are opened. The grain is poured into a concrete-lined pit. Conveyor belts at the bottom of the pit carry the wheat to elevators, where the grain is graded. For example, grain with a 15 percent protein content is used to make bagels. Wheat with a 14 percent protein content is used to make flour for rolls and buns.

A freighter pulls up to the General Mills dock for loading. Grain is poured into the ship's hold at the rate of 40,000 bushels per hour. About 14 hours later, the huge ship is filled. Crossing the Great Lakes to the General Mills milling plant in Buffalo, New York, takes about five days. At the dock in Buffalo, marine legs (huge buckets on movable belts) dip into the grain. About 20 hours later, the ship is empty. The grain is shifted to silos. It is cleaned and then sent to the mill to be ground into flour. Nothing is wasted. Even the grain's chaff and husks are used for animal feed. At the General Mills plant, the flour is bagged for shipment to bakeries and grocery stores.

Back in North Dakota, Farmer Jones and her family sit down for lunch. They eat bread from the local grocery store, which, in turn, buys the bread from a bakery that uses General Mills flour. The flour might have been made from grain raised on Farmer Jones' own fields!

➤ Ships from all over the world dock at the Port of Duluth-Superior. Boat watchers can learn to identify the type, fleet, and nationality of a boat by its shape, size, hull color, **smokestack insignia,** and flag.

➤ The port can store up to 1.8 million gallons of liquid cargo, including molasses and vegetable oil.

➤ The U.S. Army Corps of Engineers was organized in 1779. The Corps maintains locks, channels, harbors, ports, and flood-control projects on U.S. coasts and rivers. The Corps also works on a variety of construction projects across the country and around the globe.

Grain and other crops from fields in Minnesota and neighboring western states pass through the Twin Ports on their way to markets all over the world. Malt barley is transported to breweries in St. Louis and Milwaukee. Wheat, soybeans, barley, corn, and sunflower seeds are shipped in bulk to North Africa and Europe.

Altogether about 29 countries import grain from the Twin Ports. These countries include the Netherlands, Belgium, Russia, Poland, Portugal, Cyprus, Nigeria, and Mexico. A variety of wheat called durum goes to Morocco, Algeria, and Tunisia to be made into couscous, a popular North African dish. More durum wheat is shipped to Italy to be made into pasta. Spring wheat goes to many European and Middle Eastern countries to make breads and pastries. Barley is sent to Israel and Saudi Arabia.

Many other materials are shipped out of the Twin Ports. Manufactured products, such as equipment for offshore oil drilling, is sent to

Norway. Chrome ore is shipped to Sweden, and petroleum coke goes to Spain. Wood pulp from Canada and Florida is shipped to paper plants in Wisconsin, Michigan, and Ohio to be made into newsprint, toilet paper, furniture, and thousands of other timber products.

What comes into the Twin Ports by ship? Limestone quarried in Michigan passes through the port and is shipped to western Minnesota to purify beet sugar. The limestone is also an ingredient in cement and iron-ore pellets, which are used for making steel. Midwestern paper mills and oil refineries use the port to coordinate inbound shipments of new machinery and outbound traffic of their finished products.

Foreign imports include plated and coiled steel from Europe—up to 60,000 tons a year—which go to fabricating plants in Minneapolis and St. Paul. Canadian salt is used to melt ice on midwestern streets in the winter. Blue pearl granite blocks from Norway are destined for St. Cloud, Minnesota, to be made into grave memorials and monuments.

All of this trade is watched carefully by the Sea- ◀ **Running the Port**
way Port Authority of Duluth, which is a political division of the state of Minnesota, the city of Duluth, and St. Louis County. The organization is mainly an administrative body. The Port Authority does not enforce laws or regulate or control ship traffic in the harbor. And it does not collect taxes on property.

The Port Authority is active on state and local issues, working to help make people aware that the port is part of Minnesota's economic community. After all, there is more to running

Duluth's exports include timber (top), *grain* (right), *and limestone* (bottom).

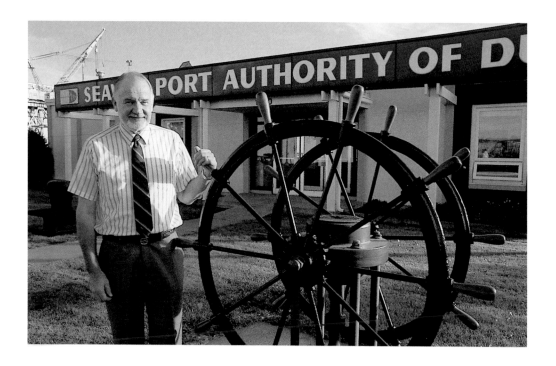

a port than loading a ship. The Seaway Port Authority of Duluth is a member of the Minnesota Ports Association. This association lobbies for state money to help improve member ports so that they stay competitive and efficient. Sometimes their efforts work. Sometimes they don't.

For years Minnesota's ports longingly eyed a port development program in Wisconsin that had started in 1980. Funded by the legislature every two years, the Wisconsin program provides up to 80 percent of project costs for harbor improvements. This upgrading stimulated a return of $17.3 million in port development for Superior, Milwaukee, and other port cities in Wisconsin that compete for Minnesota traffic. Although the Minnesota Port Development Assistance Program won legislative approval in

The Seaway Port Authority of Duluth oversees port activity and makes sure things are running smoothly.

1991, no money was authorized for projects until 1996.

In spite of such frustrations, the Seaway Port Authority of Duluth stays active on many trade fronts. Its staff assists TEAM DULUTH, which encourages new businesses to come to the city. Other members of TEAM DULUTH include the city of Duluth, the Duluth Economic Development Authority, and Minnesota Power. The Port Authority also contributes to keeping commercial traffic flowing through the community.

Port officials would like a crystal ball to help predict the future of the port. But, of course, that's not possible. There isn't much they can do to control international trade conditions.

TEAM DULUTH meets to discuss strategies for modernizing the port, such as expanding the port's facilities, exploring ways to adhere to environmental standards, and planning to keep money coming into the port.

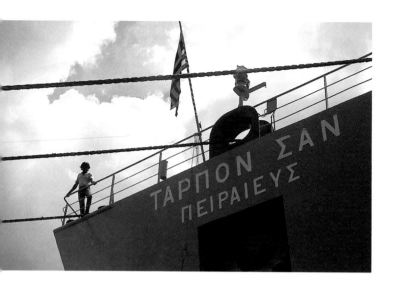

The Port of Duluth draws ships from around the world, like this ocean freighter from Greece.

So the Port Authority staff works aggressively on the local and regional levels to encourage traders to ship their goods through Duluth.

Shippers find many advantages to utilizing the **◄ Port Services**
Twin Ports. There are no local fees or taxes, only federal user fees. Rates to dock a ship are competitive. Advanced equipment often en-ables a ship to be loaded or unloaded in a day. And by storing and shipping grain and other farm products in the same climate in which they were grown, there is less spoilage.

Ship captains and crews like Duluth-Superior because the area is safe and clean, with easy access to stores, theaters, and other onshore amenities. A cab can drive up to a ship's ladder at the docks and take sailors to the Duluth Sea-farers' Center or for a night on the town, to a laundromat, or to a bookstore or movie theater.

Throughout Duluth's history, the harbor has remained important to the city. The port brings in new people and businesses and ensures that the city is internationally known. Above all, it offers jobs. More than 3,200 people—from dockworkers to customs agents—have jobs that depend on the Twin Ports. But the number of port-related occupations has been dropping since the 1970s. Where hundreds of workers once labored a decade ago, only a handful are needed today. A single computer operator, for example, can run several huge machines at the same time.

Still, many workers are needed to keep a port humming efficiently. Ship **chandlers,** for

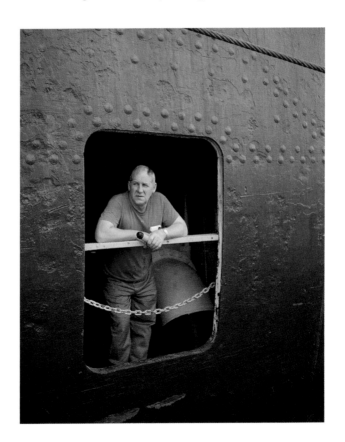

A sailor watches the docking process from a Canadian freighter.

example, act as grocery and hardware dealers for the ships. They can supply anything from engine grease to 50-pound bags of laundry detergent. They have even provided live chickens to freighters so that crews could have fresh eggs to eat. The ships use fax machines or cellular phones to place orders with the chandlers, even when the vessels are miles offshore. The supplies are then waiting dockside when the ships arrive, or they can be quickly ferried out by launch. One vessel can spend from $2,000 to $15,000 for such supplies while calling on Duluth.

Ships' agents represent a vessel owner in port. They arrange for loading and unloading.

Two crew members close the hatch doors of a cargo hold. Fewer workers than in earlier years are needed to operate automated loading and unloading machines.

The U.S. Coast Guard plays an important role in maintaining a smoothly running port. Coast Guard crews patrol and protect the harbor, enforce safety regulations, monitor pollution, and have rescue teams ready for action at a moment's notice.

They sign bills of lading, a receipt explaining what is in a cargo. If a lawyer is needed or an insurance problem arises, the agent handles the details. Agents make sure their client's vessels get fresh water, have garbage pickup, and pay tonnage taxes. The agent also prepares the captain for U.S. Coast Guard and environmental inspections.

Some workers check and maintain dock walls and pilings, to make sure the facilities stack up to inspection. Others load taconite on the giant docks or monitor water quality in the harbor.

A stevedore company supplies grain elevators and warehouses with groups of day laborers called **longshoremen.** These workers are supervised by a foreman called a walking boss. When a ship needs help loading or unloading cargo, the jobs are posted each day at the International Longshoreman's union hall.

A self-unloading ship uses a series of conveyor belts to unload limestone from a ship's cargo holds directly onto shore.

Duluth has faced great challenges since the 1980s, when extremely efficient self-unloading vessels began showing up on the Great Lakes. Conveyor belts in the holds of the ships made it easier to unload bulk cargo. Giant deck cranes quickly deposited material on the docks. The advent of 1,000-foot-long ships meant that fewer vessels holding more cargo called on the port. Even the demand for tugboats dropped. The new ships moved easily backward and forward into their berths on their own. In addition, fewer ships are being built in the United States, which means the lake freighter fleet is shrinking. Building a ship is not cheap. A sin-

◄ **The Future of the Port**

gle vessel can cost between $25 million and $60 million.

Some port officials question whether investment in port upgrades is worth it. Looking into the future, they say diminishing traffic means that Duluth needs to diversify even faster. But even with all these changes, port officials are optimistic. Trade patterns indicate that there will always be a need for a Lake Superior port. Operations may be scaled back. Technologies may change. But trade will continue.

Many ships are equipped with cranes (left) *to load or unload heavy machinery or pallets of prepackaged cargo. A tugboat* (below) *is dwarfed by the mighty ship in tow. Many ships have special equipment allowing them to dock unassisted.*

CHAPTER FOUR

THE ZENITH CITY

In the 1890s, Duluth was dubbed the Zenith City because it was on a hill, overlooking the lake. Since *zenith* means the highest, topmost, or best, the proud residents of Duluth felt the term applied to their hometown in many ways.

Barely 150 miles north of the business hubs of Minneapolis and St. Paul, Duluth is also only 60 miles from the vast iron-ore mines of the Mesabi and Vermilion Ranges. And it is easily reached from the farm areas of western Minnesota, Iowa, and North and South Dakota. This geographic advantage has helped Duluth develop into a bustling city.

A man drives a horse-drawn sleigh in the Duluth Winter Sports Festival parade (facing page). *Winter arrives early and leaves late in Duluth.*

61

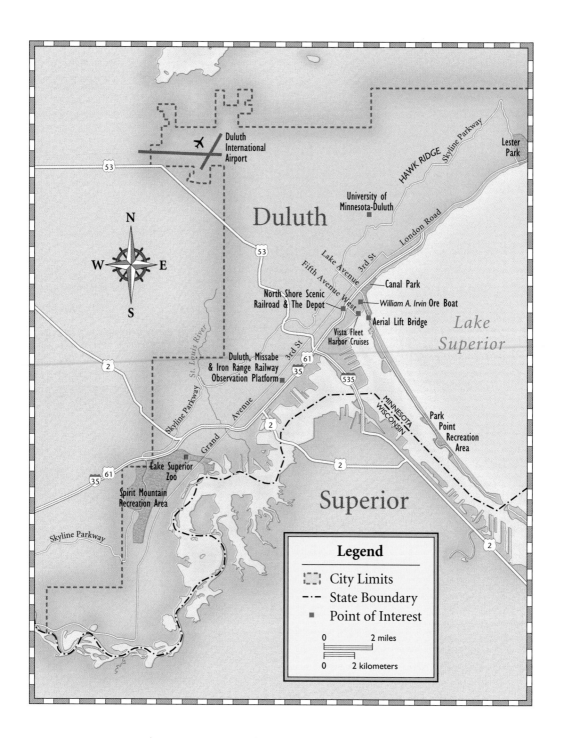

Duluth International Airport

53

N
W E
S

Duluth

HAWK RIDGE

Skyline Parkway

Lester Park

University of Minnesota-Duluth

London Road

53

Lake Avenue

3rd St.

Fifth Avenue West

Canal Park

North Shore Scenic Railroad & The Depot

William A. Irvin Ore Boat

Aerial Lift Bridge

Lake Superior

Vista Fleet Harbor Cruises

St. Louis River

2

Duluth, Missabe & Iron Range Railway Observation Platform

3rd St

61

35

535

Skyline Parkway

Grand Avenue

2

MINNESOTA
WISCONSIN

Park Point Recreation Area

35 61

Lake Superior Zoo

Spirit Mountain Recreation Area

2

Superior

2

Skyline Parkway

Legend

☐ City Limits

—··— State Boundary

■ Point of Interest

0   2 miles

0   2 kilometers

Duluth is known for its clean air and water, low crime rate, good medical care, fine educational system, and arts and recreational opportunities. Over the years, this quality of life has lured many residents to the city.

Population and Ethnic ➤ Groups in Duluth About 85,000 people call Duluth home, and almost 200,000 more live in surrounding areas of St. Louis County. Most residents—about 96 percent—are white. Just over 2 percent of the city's population are Native American. African Americans and Asians each make up less than 1 percent of Duluth's population.

The Seaway Port Authority of Duluth works hard to make sure the harbor stays clean (right). (Below) *Duluth once had a large Native population, but many modern-day relatives of these American Indians have relocated to reservations throughout Minnesota.*

Duluth has a history of welcoming immigrants. When the federal government opened the area for settlement, a rush of people from many different nations came to Duluth. In 1872 the Northern Pacific Railroad opened the Immigrant House. This hotel provided temporary living quarters for new arrivals and for people passing through town. Within a few years, up to 50 passenger trains a day were stopping at Duluth's Union Depot.

Seeking a new life, immigrants from places such as Poland, Ireland, France, Finland, Serbia, Russia, Croatia, and Slovenia poured into the North Shore region by boat and train. In the early 1900s, an Americanization committee worked hard to teach English to Duluth's newcomers and to urge them to become U.S. citizens. The city's International Institute was established in 1919 to help ease immigrants' transition to their new country.

Duluth's International Folk Festival (below and facing page) *is held every year to celebrate the international and Native peoples that make up its population.*

Visitors aboard the freighter **William A. Irvin** *(above)* *can wander the decks and see the pilot and engine rooms. The North Shore Scenic Railroad* (left) *takes tourists on an excursion along Lake Superior's waterfront.*

> Bird-watchers flock to Hawk Ridge on Skyline Parkway to see the migration of hawks and other types of birds every spring and fall.

> The observation platform of the Duluth, Missabe & Iron Range Railway is an excellent spot to watch the process of loading taconite pellets from railcars onto giant ore ships.

> Fifth Avenue West is the steepest street in Duluth. In fact, the avenue is so incredibly steep that city workers put up a handrail so pedestrians are able to pull themselves along!

> Sailor guides onboard the *William A. Irvin*, a 600-foot freighter, tell their stories about working on the Great Lakes as they lead visitors through the floating museum's engine room, pilot house, and restored staterooms.

Newcomers brought their beliefs and work ethics with them. For instance, among the many Scandinavian arrivals were thousands of Finnish socialists. They believed in community ownership of transportation, utilities, and other public enterprises. Immigrants from Finland protested for better working conditions on the Iron Range and helped organize a Duluth dockworkers' strike in 1913. This strike forced installation of safety devices on unloading equipment.

The first Slovenes arrived in the 1880s on their way to work in the mines. As early as 1907, Serbian laborers began building dam projects in northern Minnesota for the local power company. Romanians and Slavic peoples planted large gardens and set up smokehouses behind their homes. They also built meeting halls and churches, enjoyed colorful festivals, and helped other newcomers from their countries adjust to life in Duluth.

This international flavor can still be found in the Twin Ports. Greek and Polish restaurants, for example, are popular gathering places for crews from those countries. They find friends who speak their languages, newspapers from home, and familiar foods.

For many years, most of the sailors who anchored in Duluth were from Europe. Nowadays many ships arrive from Africa, Asia, and Latin America, bringing their cultures and religious beliefs. This variety of nationalities presents some challenges to the port. The Port Authority uses professional translators from the University of Minnesota at Duluth when necessary. Even the Duluth police department has officers

The Canal Park boardwalk (above) *is a perfect place to watch ships in the harbor, to get some exercise, or just to take in the scenery. The sculpture garden* (facing page) *has whimsical, elegant, and historical sculptures for visitors to enjoy.*

who are fluent in Slavic languages, Spanish, and Japanese.

Residents and visitors alike have always been drawn to Duluth's waterfront. A source of business and recreation, the Lake Superior shoreline is important to community development. A lake boardwalk is a favorite route for walkers, in-line skaters, joggers, bikers, and picnickers. The boardwalk passes through Canal Park, where sightseers gather to watch ships enter

◄ **What's Happening in Duluth?**

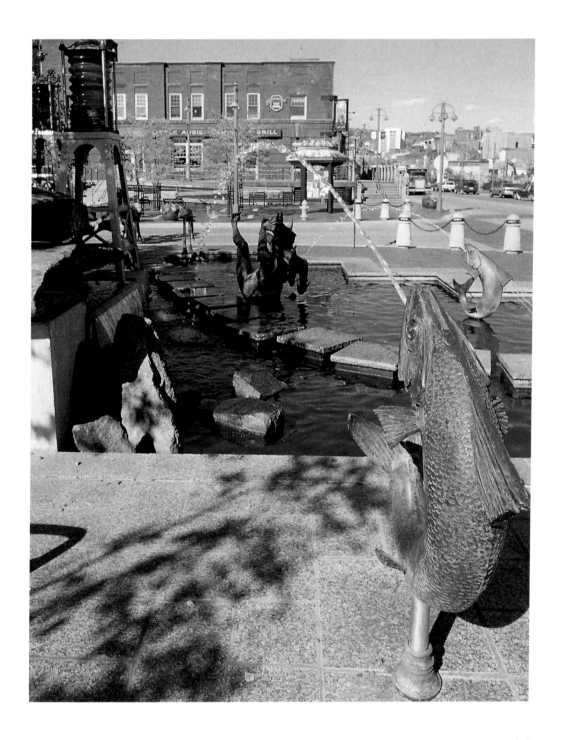

the port. A refurbished warehouse district along the waterfront holds shops and restaurants, as well as a sculpture garden.

Duluth's clean air, fresh water, and thick forests draw people to the great outdoors. In summer, nature lovers can hike along the city's eight trails, canoe the area's rivers and lakes, or go white-water rafting on the St. Louis River. Picnickers and softball players can find space to relax at any of Duluth's 105 municipal parks. The city's heavy winter snow draws downhill and cross-country skiers, as well as snowmobilers.

Skiers (above) *at Spirit Mountain take advantage of Duluth's long winter season. Autumn foliage* (below).

Duluth's Bayfront Blues Festival (top) *draws crowds of young and old alike. At The Depot* (bottom), *visitors get a dose of history, art, and technology all in one spot.*

Arts and Entertainment in Duluth ➤ Duluth is a regional center for the arts, attracting patrons to the ballet, symphony, and theater. At The Depot, visitors find four museums in one, including the Lake Superior Museum of Transportation. Here, tourists can climb on-board the earliest trains that operated in Duluth. Animal lovers can find more than 500 species of animals from around the world at the Lake Superior Zoo.

The famed Beargrease Sled Dog Marathon sets off from Duluth each January. It takes competitors about four days to complete the 500-mile loop.

Duluth also offers a variety of entertainment and annual events. Each June Grandma's Marathon draws thousands of runners to Duluth. The city's Bayfront Blues Festival in August offers 20 bands on three stages. During the chilly winter months, 30 teams of mushers race in the 500-mile Beargrease Sled Dog Marathon as part of the Duluth Winter Sports Festival. And folksingers often gather at Sir Benedict's Tavern, where flags of different nationalities are regularly rotated.

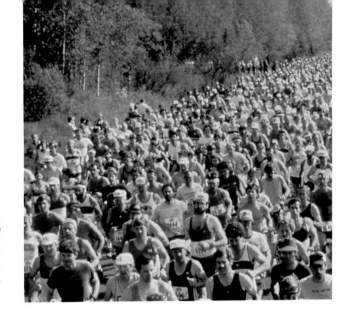

Grandma's Marathon (right) *attracts runners from around the world. Sir Benedict's Tavern* (below) *hosts folksingers who entertain diners with their tunes.*

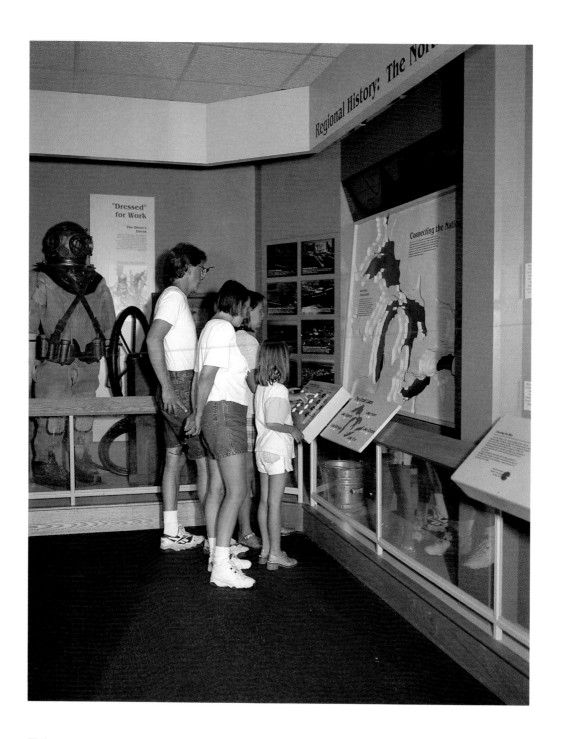

Duluth's Labor Force ➤ The waiters, clerks, and other workers who serve residents and visitors alike are part of Duluth's large service sector, which employs about 82 percent of the city's labor force. Service workers include teachers, doctors, police officers, bankers, and longshoremen and other port employees. Government workers, who make up another 5 percent of the labor force, are generally considered to be part of the service sector.

Major industries in the city of Duluth include paper mills and food-processing plants. Laborers in the manufacturing sector make up about 8 percent of the city's workforce. Masons, electricians, carpenters, and other construction workers make up about 4 percent of the labor force in Duluth, while the mining and the agriculture sectors each employ less than 1 percent of the city's workers.

To acquaint sixth-grade students with the St. Louis River and the variety of jobs related to the port at Duluth, port personnel established the River Quest program in 1993. Each spring hundreds of youngsters pile onboard the *Vista Star* excursion boat for a hands-on harbor tour. While onboard, they talk with various representatives of the public and private organizations that deal with Duluth, the St. Louis River, and Lake Superior. The students learn about pollution control, sewage treatment, Coast Guard rescue operations, commerce, piloting freighters, and a host of other topics. Inspired by what they see, some of these students may one day join the vast team of dedicated people that make the Port of Duluth-Superior one of the top ports in the United States.

In addition to harbor cruises aboard the **Vista Fleet,** *visitors at the Marine Museum in Canal Park* (facing page) *can learn about port activity and the tradition of shipping on the Great Lakes.*

GLOSSARY

ballast tank: Holds, or tanks, deep within a ship that are filled with water or other heavy substances to keep the vessel stable.

broker: An agent who acts as an intermediary between a buyer and a seller, arranging contracts of purchase and sale.

chandler: A dealer who sells supplies or equipment of a specific kind.

free trade zone: An area near a transportation hub such as a seaport or an airport where goods can be imported without paying import taxes. Foreign traders may store, display, assemble, or process goods in these zones before shipping them to the place where they will eventually be sold. The United States has about 70 free trade zones.

gantry crane: A crane mounted on a platform supported by a framed structure that runs on parallel tracks so as to span or rise above a ship for purposes of loading and unloading cargo.

hopper car: A freight car with a floor that slants downward toward a hinged door, which swings open to release bulk cargo.

icebreaker: A powerful, heavy ship with a strengthened hull (body) that breaks through ice to maintain open, navigable channels of water. Some icebreakers ride on top of the ice until the weight of the vessel crushes the ice. Other ships break through the ice by backing up and ramming into it. The most powerful icebreakers can travel through ice that is more than 20 feet thick.

lock: An enclosed, water-filled chamber in a canal or river used to raise or lower boats beyond the site of a waterfall or a set of rapids. Vessels can enter and exit the lock through gates at either end.

longshoreman: A worker who loads and unloads ships at a port.

smokestack insignia: A special marking on a ship's smokestack The insignia, a combination of geometric shapes, colored bands, letters, or logos, indicates to which company or government agency a ship belongs.

spit: A small point of land, usually made of sand or gravel, extending into a body of water.

PRONUNCIATION GUIDE

Anishinabe	uh-nih-shih-NAH-bay
Dakota	duh-KOH-tuh
Duluth	duh-LOOTH
Fond du Lac	FAHN duh LAK
Grand Portage	GRAND POHR-tihj
Huron	HYUHR-ahn
Mesabi	muh-SAH-bee
Ojibwa	oh-JIHB-way
St. Louis	SAYNT LOO-uhs
Sault Ste. Marie	SOO SAYNT muh-REE
Sieur du Lhut, Daniel Greysolon	SYUHR doo LOOT, DAN-yuhl grehs-aw-LOH[n]

INDEX

METRIC CONVERSION CHART

WHEN YOU KNOW	MULTIPLY BY	TO FIND
inches	2.54	centimeters
feet	0.3048	meters
miles	1.609	kilometers
square feet	0.0929	square meters
square miles	2.59	square kilometers
acres	0.4047	hectares
pounds	0.454	kilograms
tons	0.9072	metric tons
bushels	0.0352	cubic meters
gallons	3.7854	liters

ABOUT THE AUTHOR

Award-winning author Martin Hintz has written numerous books for young readers and hundreds of magazine and newspaper articles. Other Lerner titles he has written include *Destination New Orleans, Destination St. Louis,* and *Farewell, John Barleycorn: Prohibition in the United States.* Hintz lives in Milwaukee, Wisconsin.

ACKNOWLEDGMENTS

The author expresses his appreciation to the staff of the Seaway Port Authority of Duluth for the time and interest everyone took to explain how their agency functions. Special thanks go to Davis Helberg, executive director of the Port Authority; Sam L. Browman, marketing director; Lisa Marciniak, promotion manager; Captain Ray Skelton, environmental and government affairs director; and Andy McDonough, business development director.

Additional thanks are offered to Karl Nollenberger, administrative assistant to the mayor/city manager of Duluth; Pat Maus of the Northeast Minnesota Historical Center; Pat Labadie, director of the U.S. Army Corps of Engineers/Canal Park Marine Museum; Gerald Kimball, retired Duluth city planner; Richard W. Ojakangas and Charles L. Matsch, Minnesota geologists; and Gerald Niemi, director of the Center for Water and the Environment at the University of Minnesota-Duluth. Naturally there are many other professionals who commented on the Twin Ports' history, environmental issues, economics, and operations, as well as on the impact of the port on the broader community. The author welcomed their comments, insights, and scholarship.

Discussions on lake navigation, seamanship, and security as explained by the U.S. Coast Guard team in the Twin Ports were very helpful. Thank you, Captain Steve Gilbert, Lieutenant Scott Smith, and Senior Chief Frank Andrews. A special nod goes to retired Coast Guard Captain Gil Porter and the members of the Propeller Club. Finally the author would like to thank Marc Mansfield, director of the Duluth Chamber of Commerce; Kristi Schmidt, public relations director of the Duluth Convention & Visitors Bureau; Ray Lotte, manager of cereal and eastern grain operations for General Mills; the folks at the Duluth Public Library and the St. Louis County Historical Society; the staff of the Radisson Hotel Duluth; and the cooks and servers at all the ethnic eateries discovered on this adventure.